I0756287

my teacher's name is love

Also by Victor Marsh:

Mr Isherwood Changes Trains

Speak Now: Australian Perspectives on Same-Sex Marriage (editor)

The Boy in the Yellow Dress

my teacher's name is love

some poems for Prem by victor marsh

Clouds of Magellan Press | Melbourne

Published by Clouds of Magellan Press

www.cloudsofmagellanpress.net

ISBN: 978-0-6453531-7-4 hbk

ISBN: 978-0-6453531-8-1 pbk

'shell game' was previously published in the CG Jung Society of Queensland *Newsletter*, the *haiku* 'natural chandelier' and 'river like glass' were published in *Wild Honey*; 'high noon' appeared in *Regeneration* (Lismore Council 2003); 'crochet doilies' appeared in *Letters from the Soul* (2003); 'god/sex' published in *White Crane Journal* (2003). Some of these poems have appeared on the audio CD *Poems from a Grateful Heart* (2006) and have been read on Bay FM 99.9 (2010) and ABC local radio, Northern NSW.

Grateful thanks to Gordon Thompson of Clouds of Magellan Press; Anne Di Lauro of the CG Jung Society of Queensland; Wendy Lovejoy, Rich Neel, Troy Schmidt, and Pam Freeman for the original audio CD *Poems from a Grateful Heart.* My deep thanks to Prem Rawat can only begin to be expressed in the following poems.

contents

after rain ... 1
inner smile ... 2
inside out ... 3
nourishment ... 4
my teacher's name ... 5
losers weepers ... 6
how should I name you ... 8
undone ... 10
crochet doilies ... 11
birdsong ... 12
thistle ... 13
you know what they say ... 14
they said ... 15
stillness moves ... 16
experience is the best teacher, right? ... 18
pilgrimage ... 19
effing the ineffable ... 20
god / sex ... 21
how long? ... 22
return ... 24
the potter's wheel ... 25
transubstantiation ... 26
heart smart ... 27
life pans out ... 28
fairy tales ... 30
sensing reality ... 32
ariadne and theseus ... 33
from my exile in the drylands ... 34

37 … some haiku
38 … 'be here, now'
40 … unborn
41 … body bag
42 … hermaphrodite
44 … nuclear power
47 … giant lizard
48 … for my master
49 … ego tripping
50 … big sky
53 … chatterbox
54 … shell game
56 … home free
58 … high noon
60 … this blessèd pause
62 … I lives in my head
64 … control centre
65 … melbourne haiku
66 … listening

after rain

clouds pass after rain
sunlight falls on new green shoot
my heart now with you

inner smile

When I let go to that inner smile
that glows inside my
heartspace

it's like some sphincter
clutching tight around my
breathing

lets go

releasing peace to flow
in every corner of my
breathing

Resting in that peace
a deeper sense of trust comes
through to make its home
here

All sense of me and my
dissolves and clarity prevails
absolutely without
reason

inside out

I stretched so far outside of me
to touch the furthest edges of infinity
that universe so vast it blew my mind
to ponder a galaxy light years to cross.

Straining to know,
I left the seat of wisdom
and did not find my way back
before a half a lifetime and a lot of disappointments
passed.

I have a mirror I can use to see myself
(but it doesn't show my eyes!)
Who looks there?

My Buddha has four arms
and Christians fear I have forsaken
the Cross to worship graven images!

I sit in his lap, and
as each arm wraps me in his whole embrace.
'I' dies
and there is only Light and
Nectar infiltrates the subtle threads of
silence.

nourishment

released from this messy
busyness of human
doing

return to the
heart of being

nourished from within by
endless peace

find home …

my teacher's name

my teacher's name is
love
his heart enfolds mine
wholly

his gaze takes in my warthog
self
in all its snuffling
gruffness

and with infinite, gentle
ease
shifts my brooding hog
mind

into a better space
clarifying vision
until i see
my self
and all the world
transformed.

i look back at him in
love
and we smile together
as the wellspring of joy
bubbles
free

losers weepers

losing my way
waiting to find the thread
again

and waiting some more
(the things I do to kill the time!)

i hear from You
 and a small tremor of
            excitement stirs

reminding me i'm not
            alone

something deeper,
a more original
            self

trembles into
            being

waking from the numbed
            state
i've had her in

awaiting what?
            the readiness
of being awake is
            my reward

content now to be
            cognisant

the what and the why
            and the wherefore
don't quite cut the mustard
            now

how should I name you

I've tried to call you master
teacher, coach and guide …
My boss

Now what to say, friend?

You always seem to be the
other side of the world from me
yet here I find you are
my heart

For when I go to hear you speak you see
my heart talks straight to me
no space at all between us
despite appearances

the laws of space and physics
turned on their very heads

Bring me home I beg you
wind me in, sabotage my errant
plots that wander far away

You say: here is how
to find the heart of all existence:
listen inside, tune your head to heart's
own wavelength. That's not
so far away

Then the jumbled jigsaw tumbles
into place.
A whole world shifts

without a single element required to
change,

and long-sought Meaning
dissolves in being
home

… when love comes into
view

undone

You
fill up my senses
overwhelm me utterly
within

until i
no longer knows
who or what
this or that
in or out
you, me
end begin

You
ease heart's breath free
of that tighter sphincter, me
release beginning ending …

Where i was
You always are
this being's
home

crochet doilies

Thought
weaves fearful spaces
denser, picking over patterns fretfully
familiar
loves to knit webs tight
together
like an old lady doing crochet.

Nightly, tightly, like a spider in my brain

Your voice spins a different
yarn
softly whispers freedom's
song
unravels my most cautious
carings
spooling out fine filaments of light.

Increasingly releasing me from webs spun day and night…

Old lady's carefully constructed
cage
fragile, falls
apart.
A tissue of imaginings
crumbles mere to
dust
as my heart flutters
free.

birdsong

there, wobbling on the wire
of my neighbour's rooftop
aerial

backlit against
the early summer
sky

this young magpie riffs,
delirious with the possibilities
of joy

thistle

sometimes, the sound of Your voice is enough
to blow away the crusty shells around my heart
as easily as a puff of breeze
disperses thistle seeds

and my heart of hearts, revealed, stands clear
again and again
and again

you know what they say

They say it's merely 'neurological'
this experience of being in bliss,
that love itself's a mere brainfart!

So I ask: did they renounce sex
when they found it only physical
or denounce their self-important 'I'
opining as just an artefact of neurons firing?

Neurotic logic stems from wrong-head tuning
sounds truth for those whose ears
have lost the knack for harmony
speaks only to those lonely hearts
who've wilfully forgotten how to fly

As if this aeolian harp, my nervous system
could not be tuned to catch breath's wind
and find the sweetest music playing through my soul

As if, in emptying body, mind, all sense of me
my hollowed soul flute could
prove too dense for you
to breathe new life in me

If it's only physical, this body
and will surely die one day
I've found the secret flower that it bears

and the sacred seed which once you planted
has brought to fruit its
promise

they said

They said:

If you don't get married
settle down
have children
You'll surely die alone.

They said:
If you don't know Jesus
get saved
be born again
You'll surely go to Hell.

i said nothing
But in my heart i waited for You to come and
surely bring me home.

stillness moves

an acrostic poem

In the shadow caverns of human being
Silence speaks for me

When, withdrawn
Inside the folds of caring, the
Tugging pulse of thought subsides, my
Heart relinquishes her anxious ways, to
Idle, breathborne
Now is all the time there is and ever was

I am just a boy from Perth, but my Master
Showed me

When that gentle breath kisses my heart
Into being, I am hers;
That in perfect privacy she will take me
Home; that
Over the concave fall and
Under the convex rise of breathswell lie
Tranquillity's profoundest pools.

But why do you hide behind my eyes? You could
release me from this
endless game of hide
and seek, Mother! I'm
tired and I want to come
home. My feet are sore. I'm sure I'll get lost again:
every thought, every flicker of interest in something else
something yet to be done!

I'll keep polishing the mirror
now, an old task for a new devotee.

Between each breath
remembering how
even now I could catch your foot; if not, perhaps
a glimpse of you in there …
that you don't live in
heaven, and you won't be found in hell
even if a thousand years of telling would have you
dwelling in such unsuitable accommodations.

Oh, won't you come out once, for all time, from
under your only hiding place? Call 'Game's up!'
take me home, into your deepest heart, forever and ever …

experience is the best teacher, right?

… that's what they say.
So how come yesterday
I was in bliss
while today I banged my head the same place
I've done a million time before
and all my dreams of love have flown away?

Break the rules just one more time,
please Master?
Save me from my own forgetfulness!
Ignorance isn't bliss, I know that now
and even with the best teacher
I'll have to be a better student
than I know how
to get my lessons right
and find the path away from pain
once and for bloody all.

Meanwhile back to basics
like You showed me
allow the beads of breath in lungtime's *mala*
to bring this crazy me-self to a safer place
and learn to Rest-In-Peace in life, not death

Unless this 'I' could simply die
and let love fly, unbridled
released from the cage of worry,
and obsessive little
rituals it likes to call a life.

pilgrimage

I hear of those who go on pilgrimage
to see God's birthplace, a promised land
a Buddha's tooth.

I don't travel far to meet my Maker.

Look behind your eyes and know
that priests and pontiffs
are no closer to the truth than you are.

We draw our breath from the same source
What causes that gives life
for all our arrogance.

If you would know your own true home
Find the place where breath is born.

effing the ineffable

with apologies to Sam Beckett

whoever has heard this song that rings within the silence
or the hush of a wave that skids upon an inner shore

or glimpsed the glow of pearls within the darkness
or felt subtle movement pulse in perfect stillness

or perceived the power of presence as the void

where none has climbed no steps or ladders
to revive their union in an emptiness of self

knows a bliss not snagged or caught with nets of thought
nor known with any organ

before 'I am', this is, now,
forever and before …

god / sex

They're arguing about the sex of God!
(Or, should I say the 'gender'?)

Damn' fool question, that.

I reckon God/Goddess makes love
in the rise and fall of breath
and I am the fruit of that
perfect Union.

how long?

How long will you go on like this
concealing yourself behind the world
showing yourself only obliquely
as though one day I might be subtle enough to
penetrate your disguise. Fat chance that!

I'd like to hear you clear your throat
stamp a foot, insist on full attention once in a while.

Yet if you did, I know I'd be the first to run away
frightened, wouldn't I?
So in your wisdom you leave things just as they are
and waiting, hide until I collect enough sense
(or is it bitter life experience)
to finally seek you out.

I who thinks that love lives on the outside
who thinks I must have carelessly lost the better
half of me somewhere else.
I, who seek out love with other crazy beggars
suffering from the same delusions.

When all the while I should've learned, through
so much trial and error
that my heart is the doorway to my homeland,
the principal organ of perception
(physiology be damned),
allowing the whole puzzle to jigsaw
for a moment into place

and all my anxious queries fly home
like pigeons, cooing murmurs of contentment
to replace my anguished cries.

So I beg you, Master, don't leave it up to me
show me where that lives, the one I lost.
Tune my nervous system to the
ultra finest frequency, UFF
and lock it in there.

Until each pulse becomes a beat
to bring me into line
each breath a swing to ride in;
and every single moment of this
tiny, finite life form
transformed, becomes divine.

return

I used to run around, try to cram it all in,
thinking life there'd never be the time
to know what life could give me.

Human doing!

Now I know that to taste life fully
is a matter, merely, of deepening my capacity
to be more fully here.

When I slows down
each moment spreads
and nothing can contain what
overflows my heart.

the potter's wheel

I threw a pot on a wheel one day
Or at least a lump of clay.
Under my teacher's hands
that clay would rise and form a shape
be all that it could be

under mine a stubby, two-inch ashtray.

My more ambitious try rose high
promising great things
before unwinding down.
The same momentum that had driven it up
undid it wholly.

Before he raises the pot
all the power of the potter's arms
tame centrifugal force
to hold the centre firm, centripetally.

My teacher is kind and makes me
repeat that lesson every single day.

No more pots 'til I get it right.

transubstantiation

Yes, take your wafer,
sip your wine
By all means do that with the very best respect
that's due to ritual.
Chant your mantram, count your rosary
light your candles, keep your hope alive
with your difficult mystical practices.

But have you noticed all the while
this living gift (so often overlooked):
this current breath, right now
consecrates this very moment

blessing you into being?

How much respect is due to that?

heart smart

O, my patient heart!

You're like a mother.
Children come and snuggle in your lap
run away to play …

You watch calmly as they
jump up and
down
Scream, shout
strut some stuff
Come back, suckle
run off to play again.

Go away, come back again,
go away come back again
go away …

life pans out

Life pans out in
        deadly, linear
                regularity
flattening all affect in deadening ennui.

All feeling bound up at
        the temporal
                edge of being.

Pausing, even stopping altogether
        allowing that axis to be
                pierced by a vertical
                        nowness

time itself might stop.

The garrulous narrator then without
        fuel for his incessant
                fabrications,

and for a change
        not threatened by
                stillness, nor entranced
                        by his own ideas

accepting the stillness of caesura
        a pulse is felt.
                The original sound
                        resounds

Breath itself invites one
home to nothing
to expire
in not being
me.

fairy tales

I probably shouldn't let on
but I'll tell you what I'm plotting.
You know those silly stories
where a fairy grants three wishes
which somehow stupid folk will always throw away?

Ha! I know how to trick that genie
– if I ever got the chance –
into granting me the single wish
those fools have never thought of.
I'd only need one: that all my wishes
ever be fulfilled.
Clever dick, eh?

Ah dammit! There I've told you.

But while I think of it …

Maybe I know why that's never going to happen.

Given my monkey mind's restless
endless wandering, I'd rave a thousand
useless universes into play!
What mayhem then should give me pause
from wishful thinking.

Perhaps I'll wait then until
I'm wise enough to know just what to ask for

and in the meantime
get to know the one gift underlying
all my dreaming.

The one that makes the countless universes
and my little life, too, come
into play.

sensing reality

silence speaks for me

i listen with my heart now
taste with my eyes
see with my ears
loving You breath by breath

Lord, you didn't warn me
how You could bring such sweet
confusion, and save me
wholly

ariadne and theseus

Foreseeing he'd still be lost
her golden lover-man
in the labyrinth's endless ways
she impressed her plan upon his brain:

'Despatch the Bull, my half brother
with this short sword
then come back to me, lover
following this thread.

'Tie this ball of twine
at the entrance when you begin.
Unwind it along behind you
as you enter into the maze.'

*

I see this, my bull-body, dead, alas!
Need I die too?

You left your thread
for me to follow, too, dear friend
It's folded in my breath
so that in the end I may come
home to you.

from my exile in the drylands

In Broome, a coastal town in the
northwest of my so-called 'home state'
West Australia
the tide goes out for miles, you know?

Pearl luggers moored at the jetty there
would sit, awkwardly, on cracked mudflats
high and dry
and tourists stroll by with impunity.

But when the tide, compelled, turned
shoreward, an obedient ocean flowed
surely back in to float those boats
upright again.

Everything just as it should be.

Through years in exile, inured, I
grew used to a cracked, dry feeling
where a heart might be.

Hope had almost gone for me.
I muttered bitterly: Truly is this all?
Until I heard from you, sweet friend

(and not a second to soon …)

Then another kind of tide would come
flooding in, pouring this being peace full
setting his heart bobbing

afloat, anew.

*

I may rest, assured this tide won't turn,
recede to leave me dry, sighing for love's
faint breath—as in geography it might—

thanks due to you!

For your rule of law cancels out the tidal
tug of moon's mere pull, releases me from
exile in the bad dry lands of fear

brings me back to that real 'home state'
where peace gives birth to each and every swell of birth

and all my sighs return to love.

That's not situated in the North, no
nor South, nor East, nor West, I'll add.
My home state's no place where a body

squats its butt upon the earth.

Even being still, 'I' roams free in inner
skies, and all the trillion stars of heaven's
heartlands are countless beads of rosaries
chanting endless praise for you.

Even if they give you all the keys to every
little city of the wide known world, with honours,
I figure the one that counts

is that key you lent so kindly
when you blessed the possibility of liberty
even thus to me.

some *haiku*

natural chandelier
accident of web and dew
adorns the morning

river like glass
reflects the sky
fish among the clouds

wave skids in, retreats
seabird skitters back and forth
eye alert for pipis

muggy air lies still
cicadas buzz, midday
heat mugs bushland dry

'be here, now'

'Be here, now,' they always say! How did good advice, alas,
become a mere cliché? Will you be damned, Ram Dass, to
have sown this irritant so widely?

You smuggled it from its alien origins into the West, in the
Sixties – thwarted the forces of Border Security – disguised it
as a book and spread it about, willy bloody nilly,
a New Age Johnny Appleseed.

But is this a foreign, Hindu seedling, merely?
I don't know. I'm no expert on cross-cultural-ethnobotany!

One thing I've found, though, is that if I have ever,
howsoever, chanced to find myself in the aforesaid 'now',
it hasn't been a matter merely of putting on the brakes,
successfully arresting my (aging) childish urgency from
rushing on, onwards, ever onwards,

that the real effect is not a retardation, then
– what use frustration? That's not the way to go! –
No, it's not an arrest to please some perverse wrong-headed,
jailer, in service to the mind police.

When I slow down – however that occurs – miraculously
come to rest content here (wherever), now (whenever),

The horizontal axis of time is interrupted, adroitly
intersected by a vertical axis.

Rather than pressing forward then, time's false bottom
drops right out, and 'now' becomes eternity.

Hear that sound?

What border guard would recognise *this* concealment!
He'd have to arrest me, and time itself.
And where's the jail would hold me,
were I to find my home this way?

unborn

A part of me was never born
still floats in amniotic
bliss

Furled within the ancient womb of being
my soul, at home,
resides in peace
and love herself draws breath for me …

So if I laugh when you
ask me, Mother:
'Come home,
aren't you sad
to be alone?'

I'm always home, you know:
heart is where the home is,
Ma!

body bag

this body bag

– skinful of shit and blood and bones –

how can it house the deepest yearning, seedbed of
heartspace bliss;

what is this mystery here?

hermaphrodite

Hermes, and Aphrodite, the Gods' Messenger and the Goddess of Love herself united to create Hermaphrodite, who carries within the twin poles of being, two sides of self, yin and yang as one, male and female energies entwined within the flow of breath, which pulses out to form the universes spinning free,

Great Exhalation exaltation

And pauses a moment, suspended out of time, before a gentle ebb returns and swells to form a river rushing back towards the dark intensities, contracting, powerful into tempered potency, held in wait, samurai poised with razor sword …

Restraint valued far above angry reaction, sharp attack forsworn to sit
all poised in vigilance …

Until, almost by accident one day, samurai hooks into gentle resting breath and finds the pulse of peace hidden, encoded within his breath.

His extreme maleness melts, intermingled with honeyed warmth of blissful mothering love, making him whole within.

Holy embrace of mother father god, my boy-and-girlness bleeding into one another with nothing left to show but love.

My Teacher showed me the way through the maze of being, left me this thread to follow, back along the way, silently whispering its call within my subtle breath, a resting place, neutral to all my doings, human being home.

nuclear power

Warmed by several days of so-called
'selfless' service,
thawed out
I came to your feet
(as I had done a hundred time before).

Dancing through the queue
when I came to you
it was as though you shrank!

(Sometimes you grow ENORMOUS
and I quake!
What kind of lenses
do I need to wear
to keep you in focus?)

On this day you shrank
and revealed yourself to be
the most intense, atomic kernel;
the microscopic pearl of
brilliant love
residing secretly,
concealed intimately
at the heart of every molecule
that this universe is made of !

(And I'm the hardened nut who never
hallucinated, mind,
even on half a dozen tabs of LSD!)
Is this how it all hangs together?

Now I know what they mean
when they refer to
nuclear
power!

Yes! You are the pearl of love that
generates the universes into being
the very seed of life
the blueprint for a universe
of love.

And that seed was hidden mysteriously
in my heart, too!

But this only came to life in me
When i met You.

I should be careful, though.
For were I to claim to see
these secret things
they'll call me mad,
arrest me,
declare me incoherent,
incompetent

not fit to mingle with the people
of this world.

If that became the case, then where
this man should live?
In an asylum for the blissfully
insane?

(Where are those spectacles that would keep
me straight?)

Would it cause another outrage, then,
were I to ask:
May i hang in there, with You …
… eternally?

giant lizard

One day, when crashing through the bush –
I would have said 'walking', but when I
settled down upon a log I heard, compared to
'quiet', that my every move was noisy.

So, when I stopped, and settled on that
log, I slipped inside a moment that
tipped me inside out …

A simple act, to sit upon a
log, undoing all my going to
let my breath come back to me …

Quiet now, I notice rustling here and there.
Dragonflies hover, birds chirrup,
insects scuffle in the underbrush,
a wagtail darts to check the coast is clear,
a thousand ants hustle on about their business:

All this emerging after my noisy intrusion had
parted the wave and gone.

There's little left of me now, save a
lingering grin, when a giant lizard masterfully
scales a tree trunk, flicks out his
tongue, surveys his own domain.

Through his eyes, I see the world anew.

for my master

I heard such talk, impressive tales
Of sadhus, Avatars
God made men!

And I waited at my gate
Dreaming of a super hero

Meanwhile, you came to clean my house …
Live-in servant,
            room-mate,
            confidant,
            friend
and in the clean up:
            lift your feet,
            move your butt
            hold onto this,
            let go of that

All the while, and ever so slyly
You slid me into spaces
            in my heart
that make me swoon!

Who'll sing your praises?

ego tripping

You sit squat in the cockpit of
ego, as if the whole damned world
passes by just for your review.
Do you approve?
Who *know*s what faults you find in
each and every one of us!

Did you ever think what gives us breath
to be and do might pause
and then where would
you *be*? Eh?

As for *me*, on the other hand …
ahem! well I …

Perhaps we ought to get together.
We'd make a fine
coupling.

big sky

It really shook me down, you know,
to hear this big blue sky
is just a pretty, shared
delusion!

This shell under which I
sheltered, an optical illusion
created by some refractory
angle of the light!

While the real picture immensely,
deeply dark and fathomless
goes on forever

It really did my head in!

'Oh it's just that we turned away from
the sun for half a day
that's all', they told me
as if that should be some
comfort

A few words threaded together
some concepts posing,
authoritatively, as if Science
with a capital sigh explained
it all away.

'Are you afraid of the dark, silly boy?
When I looked up at the cerulean
delusion, knowing now
that it conceals the actual
state of affairs, the
deepest darkness

I couldn't take comfort in the
puerile security blanket
they offered me

How is it I don't fall off the
geosphere, especially as I
live in the southern
hemisphere and might fall into no-
thing, then?

'Gravity' was supposed to be my
balm, a salve to soothe the
existential angst that riddled
my days and nights!

It really did my head in!

And NASA's space probes
are supposed to give some
comfort, apparently?

It really did my head in!

It all depends on your point of
view. You showed me
an alignment that brings
together the me, the anxious 'I'
and all the rest …

For the focal point is some-
where behind my eye/'I' and
I needs to go inside and find
its root, not 'I' for the
universe (confusing word,
that!)

chatterbox

There's a chatterbox lives in my head.
Sometimes she sounds all sweet and
reasonable. At other times she shows
her nasty side, picking on this person
or that, finding fault on every side.

She likes me to think of her as my friend.
The world would be a far better place
were it only arranged better, according to her.
But then what would she have to complain about?

If she thinks I'm getting tired of her nastiness
she'll try to interest me in the world of make believe.
She knows her duty better than I know mine.
How can I get past this thicket of thought
and reach the other side, I ask, where peace resides?
And she'll do endless riffs on that.

Won't you ever just bloody shut up, say I,
stamping an irritated foot.

I'm just doing my job, she claims
Why don't you do yours?

shell game

Inside an egg, a chicken grows
and grows, so soon
that shell has lost its power
to shelter,
now a prison tight
become.

The growth of life
itself
puts pressure on that shell
inside, insists it
give way
crack! split! wide open,
release the life
within.

For little chick perhaps
that birth's
a death;
worlds collapsing,
all hell breaking
loose!

But big mother hen
awaits,
clucks comfort and encouragement
and
after weeks of warmth
invites the chick into
a wider world,

knows where grubs are caught,
water drunk
and grain to fill the gullet,
a sun to warm
and stretch
and COCK-A-DOODLE in
if he would just
emerge!

home free

Reading a depressing novel
(by a prize-winning author no less)
pushing myself reluctantly on
through its unhappy wasteland
to find out what happens
with those miserable
creatures.

Seven difficult pages further I
plod. Then, for the *n*th time I put
the book down, wipe my bum, flush,
and go to meditate.

I really shouldn't be surprised, but
(sitting now on that same backside)
beneath the familiar dry, soulless
landscape
I find in here, again
        this lake of
        solace …
always.

A shocking fact: it doesn't draw
attention to itself, but as long as
I am looking for completion,
outside, I discover this vast lake
of comfort may be supporting me
        completely,
        always, even as its
        nourishment
goes untapped.

The way home starts right here,
in this place
at this time
Now.

high noon

… in which the anxious poet, disturbed by the imminent arrival of yet another anniversary of his birth, peers nervously into the mirror and is shocked to find that reflecting surface speaking back, unbidden, but nonetheless addressing unspoken fears. Astonished, he is admonished thus …

Wake up! Wake Up! No time to do your make-up
Hurry, you'll be sorry when your time has passed.
The sun's rays are shining, it's the middle of the day
While you're sleeping dreams are keeping all this love at bay.

Soon, all too soon, there'll only be a moon
The palest imitation of what we saw at noon.

White hairs are pushing last signs of youth aside.
Remember as you slumber how your soul had cried:
'The world's a pretty prison, I need to find the Lord!
If pleasure were the answer, how then could I be so bored?'

Soon, all too soon, there'll only be a moon
The palest imitation of what we saw at noon.

What water have you swallowed,
how have you slaked your thirst?
Have you drunk from the shallows now
to find there's only dirt?
Water in the desert will soon dry up
And pleasure's fancy promise turn to sand in your cup.

For soon, all too soon, there'll only be a moon
The palest imitation of what we saw at noon.

As your body starts to crumble,
will your heart's hopes take a tumble?
When your flesh is all decay, it's too late then to pray
When hungry maggots crawl there'll be no more tears to bawl.

> For soon, all too soon, there'll only be a moon
> The palest imitation of what we saw at noon.

Feed your deepest longing,
know which world that you belong in.
You're the driver, not the car, before you go too far
The crankshaft and the axle and the engine fall apart!

> For soon, all too soon, there'll only be a moon
> The palest imitation of what we saw at noon.

So now, while there's time, go in search of a heart
That's pumping only loving with no ending nor start.

> For soon, all too soon, there'll only be a moon
> The palest imitation of what we saw at noon.

That'll cost you the price of the rest of your life
But you pay that anyway, at the end of the day
No matter what they say …

> For soon, all too soon, there'll only be a moon
> The palest imitation of what we saw at noon.

this blessèd pause

Getting older brings more need for caution, I find
especially in the moment-to-moment
management of this physical vehicle,
my body.

A turn too fast can lead to
serious accidents, with long-term
consequences, alas.

On the other hand, if I pause,
even briefly, to recognise the intention
that led to the shift
and *then* move
(with all my wits about me)
this wee pause subtly broadens my
frame of reference and

And I notice more, you see.
And this insignificant shift certainly leads
to fewer shocking stumbles!

Even more so
the deeper pause (some call it
'meditation') – which shifts intention
from *doing* –
to return with meticulous apprehension
and spend some time to look, or listen
into the always present, but scarcely
noticed, zone of *being* itself …

Aah! That simple switch may bring rich rewards indeed.

Perhaps I didn't have the time before
in my enthusiasm for doing more
to gift myself the best of pausing,

stepping back from reaction
before offering my two cents worth

and learn to listen, and
hear more,
inside and out!

Is this one (secret) gift of growing so-called 'old'?

I lives in my head

problematically physicalising subjective positionality

I might have thought I'd have coherent thoughts by now
Were you to listen to what comes from my vocal
apparatus sometimes
fully formed
you could be fooled into believing there's a narratological
coherency to my mental processes
moments of grace, even

but how would you theorise the 'I' for this context, or the
'my', for that matter?

so, why are you writing a book?
that's matt. he thinks I can't see the sneer behind him
smiling.
(there'll be tears before bedtime)

I'm a rag and bones man, head's a bloody mess
scatterspray for thinking causes much distress

I was thinking I'd make some sense one day
but the days have come and gone and the one who I
was waiting for I must have missed
while I was paying attention to something else
somebody else
somebody else's
body

man
who lives
inside this
head?

some bodies have the bloom on the skin still
wear it defiant over skull

I'd take that any day to crepey grey
would that I could trade it for coherency?

by any objective standard of measurement I'm mad
collecting obsessing dreaming thinking connecting missing
an assemblage of entities posing as I

Ah me, Ah my!
Did I come here just to die?

control centre

There's an App available on
my very modern phone,
inviting me to play 'calming
background sounds', I see,
'directly from Control
Centre'.

Such wonders there to hear!

I wonder now should I go hunting for
such a miracle among the byways
offered within this complicated
digital device

(which is always getting lost …)

Or shall I stay here connected
with my original 'control' centre
not so very far away
and settle comfortably within:
within inside, like a mother hen
nestling upon her clutch of eggs

hatching fields of bliss and love ?

melbourne ***haiku***

slate clouds hang like sheets
slick cars slash the darkened road
late folk hurry home

listening

Sometimes I surrender into the stream
of music I loved from distant pasts
finding my way back to hidden comforts
called up from mostly random genres …

These days I tend to bask more in
the silence; this ancient treasure that's
really golden, I've heard it said.

The love I find here does little for
my social life but the deepest discovery
blooms and pulses in private space

and emptiness is its own reward.

Also by Victor Marsh, from Clouds of Magellan Press

The Boy in the Yellow Dress (2014)

Perth in the 1950s. After being caught wearing his mother's yellow dress, young Victor had to hide any tendency towards gender inappropriate behaviour. But his interest in dancing and theatre (and mooning over Rudolph Nureyev on the telly) were bound to make the facade collapse at some point …

'If ever a memoir captured the Zeitgeist, it's this one … Wise, funny, surprising at every turn … More than a portrait of growing up gay, it chronicles the wild search for meaning of an entire generation.' — Amanda Lohrey

Mr Isherwood Changes Trains: Christopher Isherwood and the search for the 'home self' (2010)

For forty years, British expatriate writer Christopher Isherwood was a student of a guru from the Ramakrishna Order. In *Mr Isherwood Changes Trains*, Victor Marsh details the life search for a 'home self' that found expression in later works by Isherwood, such as *My Guru and His Disciple* and in what it is seen as Isherwood's finest novel, *A Single Man.*

'At last an intelligent appreciation of Chris and his work, as well as a proper understanding of him as both a writer and Vedantist.' — Don Bachardy

'… remarkably incisive because it stretches the borders of Isherwood scholarship, and absolutely necessary because it places gay men at the very heart of the religious journey.' — Dr Donald L. Boisvert, Department of Religion Concordia University, Montreal.

www.victormarsh.com

www.ingramcontent.com/pod-product-compliance
Lightning Source LLC
LaVergne TN
LVHW101320110826
845152LV00016B/159/J

* 9 7 8 0 6 4 5 3 5 3 1 7 4 *